To dad

I think you will enjoy this
book, at least I hope you
will. Love as always
Donna   '97.

THE TOUCH OF HIS HAND

THE TOUCH
OF
HIS HAND

Dare to be love in a world that does not know how to love
CHARLES DE FOUCHAULD

PAT O'LEARY

MERCIER PRESS

MERCIER PRESS
PO Box 5, 5 French Church Street, Cork
and
16 Hume Street, Dublin

Trade enquiries to CMD DISTRIBUTION,
55a Spruce Avenue, Stillorgan Industrial Park, Blackrock, Dublin

© Pat O'Leary, 1996

ISBN 1 85635 168 8

10 9 8 7 6 5 4 3 2 1

A CIP record for this book is available from the British Library.

DEDICATION

FOR MY WONDERFUL FAMILY AND FRIENDS WHO HAVE SHOWN ME HOW HE
COMES TO US THROUGH EACH OTHER.

ACKNOWLEDGMENTS

Some of the material in this book was previously published in *The Examiner*
and *The Irish Catholic*.

Every effort has been made to trace the owners of copyright material and
it is hoped that no copyright has been infringed. If we have inadvertently
infringed any copyright we apologise and will make the necessary correction
at the first opportunity.

Printed in Ireland by Colour Books Ltd.

CONTENTS

BEYOND LONELINESS, DARKNESS AND SUFFERING
THERE IS SUNSHINE, JOY AND FREEDOM FROM FEAR
IN AND THROUGH ...

FOREWORD

True spirituality is about a relationship, a friendship with a person – the author of love Himself. It is a challenge that is nurtured and explored on a daily basis through the ups and downs, nuts and bolts, joys and sorrows of life.

It is not something apart, something reserved for certain days or special occasions. The Creator of the universe cannot be confined to a box, allowed to emerge only for specific purposes and occasions. Neither can He be confined by the limits of our human thinking to a concoction derived from our desires and fears. He is much larger than that.

Faith is the belief that someone infinitely kind and caring is there, every second of the day, in the mist of all our struggles and strivings, ready to comfort and console, to carry us through the dark times, willing and wanting only the best for us and loving us with an unconditional love that never gives up, never grows weary, never loses confidence in us.

If we reach out and clasp His hand and hold it tightly, the fears and sorrows of life can never overwhelm us. His love and care is always there, encouraging, consoling, guiding – sharing our joys and easing our sorrows. It shines most magnificently through the storms and dark tunnels, its brilliance leading us out into the light again. He is in the eye of every storm. His compassion is the face of every kindness and all the goodness we encounter in those we meet.

He asks us to walk in His way of love. That is the way that suits us best, because we were created from love and love is the harmony of our being. 'Mo Chridecan' (My Little Heart) was the name the old Irish monks called Him – it is my favourite name for the most precious friend of all ...

THE TOUCH OF HIS HAND IS
The word of encouragement that lifts our spirits and puts a
    spring in our steps again when we're feeling downcast
    and low.

The cheery smile that changes the colour and flavour of a drab, grey day.

The gift of laughter and tears.

All the goodness and kindness that we meet every day.

The comfort, love and loyalty of friends – the heart of all friendship.

The tenderness and loving care of the sick, the handicapped and the elderly.

The unique and special gift of every child.

The innate goodness and challenging honesty of young people.

The courage that champions injustices, defends the defenceless, the marginalised and the poor.

The unwavering love that erases all fear.

The strength that gives us confidence to carry on when life's hurts and disappointments cause us to falter and lose hope.

The consolation that eases the sufferings of those burdened with the heavy cross of terminal illness.

The chink of sunlight that seeps through when our dreams and hopes lie crushed and broken.

The heart of the heroic compassion that reaches into the depths and crevices to share another's grief and pain.

The sensitivity that explores deeply the suffering of humanity, and the 'tears of things'.

The little miracles and serendipities of everyday life.

The faith that inspires us to travel on blindly when we can't seem to find the way.

The gentle kindly people who spread joy and happiness about.

The altruistic people who devote themselves totally to the care and service of those who are most in need.

The hope that brings new life to one who has lost sight of the wonder and promise that life holds.

All the beauty of nature. The warmth and promise of summer sun; the clear awesome beauty of winter snow, the rustic gold of autumn, the bright promise of spring, the splendour and might of the sea, the grandeur of mountains, the dew of every dawn, the sweet song of the birds ...

The all-embracing, unconditional love and beauty of the One who lay down His very life for love of you and me.

LOVE

LOVE

THERE IS GOOD NEWS ...

There is someone who weeps when you weep.

There is someone who smiles when you smile.

There is someone very close when you feel lonely and broken inside.

There is someone urging you on through the trials and storms of life.

There is someone who calms your fears.

There is someone who carries you when you feel unable to go on.

There is someone who will never betray or abandon you.

There is someone who is always kind.

There is someone who is unable to stop caring for you.

There is someone who is sensitive to your every pain

There is someone who watches out for you.

There is someone who knows what is best for you.

There is someone who believes in you.

There is someone who knows you are uniquely special.

There is someone who will always be your friend.

There is someone who walks beside you.

There is someone who wants your love and trust.

There is someone who *loves you.*

DEAR DAUGHTER ...

A mother's letter to her daughter on the occasion of her graduation

On this special day, which marks a major milestone in your life, I want to let you know how very much you are loved and cherished. I may have failed, for many reasons, to let you know this, and so today I want to share with you the thoughts and feelings that are in my heart.

When you came into the world on that lovely spring morning, you brought with you a precious ray of sunshine which has permeated my life ever since. You arrived with a smile, happy to be here, and that is so typical of you – you love people and you love life.

You were only a very little toddler, hardly able to speak, when you tottered in from the garden one day holding something in your little fist. 'Look Mummy, look butiful flower, butiful colour.' I looked and saw the flower which you selected as the most beautiful in the garden – a dandelion!

That was the first of many glimpses I have had of your sensitive artistic nature, which always looks beyond what the world may dismiss as a 'weed'. As far as you are concerned there are no weeds, only beauty waiting to be discovered! You tend to see only the best both in people and in nature.

We have shared many joys and sorrows throughout the years. Early on, it was just the grazed knees, childhood illnesses and fears to be kissed and soothed away. More complex situations emerged during the adolescent years. I had to learn to trust more and to pray more!

Yes, of course we have had our disagreements and tiffs, but they have been few. We both have a healthy respect for the other's strong, stubborn streak! I have tried to teach you the values and standards which I hold and believe in through practice and example rather than preaching. I have tried to be fair and to listen to your hopes and dreams and to try to understand the differences between your generation and mine.

As you receive your parchment today, which is your passport to the course in life you have chosen to follow, I feel very proud of you. Proud of your achievement, because of the discipline and sheer hard grind which it entailed, but, as you know, success in examinations or in any other field, has never been the yardstick of my love and belief in you.

What makes me intensely proud is the beautiful, kind and caring person that I am privileged to call my daughter, who will never be so intent in pursuing her own goals in life, as to forget to reach out a hand of kindness and friendship to anyone who may be in need.

Please remember that I will always be there for you, whether you need a word of encouragement or a shoulder to cry on. Every day I will ask the One who placed you in my care and His Blessed Mother to guide and protect you from harm.

And if I fail to hide the tear which will, inevitably, fall, please don't be upset, it will just be the voice of that part of my heart which will always belong to you.

UNSUNG HEROES

A person can be deemed a hero because of one heroic deed performed on behalf of another. But heroism is not confined to wartime activities or specific heroic deeds. There are many people who live heroic lives quietly and courageously. Most of these will never hit the headlines, yet when we meet them, they inspire us with their courage, unselfishness and tenacity to see the heights to which people are capable of excelling. Our society very much needs to look at the lives of these 'unsung' heroes. I'm sure you know one or two, I would like to introduce you to one that I have met.

My hero's name is Jimmy. He is 12 years old and was born without legs. I met him at a children's hospital in Dublin where he spends a lot of his time. It would be very difficult to describe the gifts with which he has been endowed, but he has the most captivatingly beautiful personality I have ever encountered.

'A pure ray of sunshine,' said the nurse, when I spoke to her about Jimmy. 'He just loves everybody, and spends his time doing what he can to cheer up the other children, and keep them happy.'

Jimmy's day is spent going from bed to bed in his wheelchair, peeling oranges, picking up toys and playing with the children in cots, taking comics to and fro, just doing anything he can to help lighten everybody's day. He never speaks of his own pain, or discomfort, nor does he mention the fact that he misses being away from home so often – it is obvious that he does, because he tries to phone there as often as possible. He comes from the country so his family cannot see him very much when he is in hospital.

One day he asked me what I thought he should do when he grows up? 'Exactly what you are doing now Jimmy,' I replied. 'The greatest need in our world today is the need for people like you who spread love around.'

But, I know that Jimmy does not have a very long life expectancy, which is so often the case with the 'special' people of this world. It's as though the Lord only allows them to stay for a short time, so that we can catch a tiny glimpse of His love shining out of the weakest and littlest of His creatures, before taking these precious people home.

❤

A Tribute to the Elderly

They also serve who only stand and stare

They sit on a long bench, a row of spectators, calmly watching the drama which is taking place about them. 'Busy people' dash to and fro, some with laden trolleys, others manoeuvring small children. An odd 'stray' child manages to break away and stands crying bitterly until found again. The briefcase, pin-striped 'brigade' whiz past at an alarming rate! Life is full of excitement for these people. They are involved and needed, they have something to contribute to this drama. But what about the spectators – who are they and why are they not in-cluded in the acting out of this drama? Why are they being ignored?

These are the people in their 'twilight' years, who in fact have a great deal to contribute. The wisdom they have acquired going through life is very much esteemed and sought after in other cultures. They have learned a great deal about 'coping skills'. The crosses which they have experienced have taught them patience and tolerance. They are courteous and gracious – virtues which are so badly needed in our society today. They are great listeners and give generously of their time. They have a special affinity with young people, and tend to have a uniquely warm understanding of their struggles and strivings.

Ghandi said that the sign of a healthy society is the respect it has for its elderly. In many eastern and, what we term 'third world' countries, older people are revered and honoured for the depth of wisdom they hold.

We have a great deal to learn from these cultures in this respect, for we are very much the poorer for our short-sightedness. For, just as the youth are the root of society, the elderly are truly the gold – very precious and special 'treasures'.

ONLY PEOPLE MAKE YOU CRY

One of the most common means through which we can hurt and injure one another is through the misuse of the gift of speech and, to a greater or lesser degree, most people are guilty of this. The 'wagging' tongues, snide remarks, pleasantries in front of people and poison behind their backs. Group conversation often targets a victim for the purpose of criticising him/her, and everybody joins in for the kill. It seems to be something in our human nature, a type of sport almost, like belonging to the same club.

The most damaging thing we can do to another person is to spread scandal about them, taking their character. St Paul reminds us of the seriousness of this and aligns scandal mongering with the murder of an individual! To try to repair the damage which can be caused by the spread of scandal, we are given the example of spreading the contents of a bag of feathers over a hillside and then trying to collect each feather and put it back into the bag again! Impossible!

In lesser ways, when we would lash out through bad temper, impatience/irritability or whatever, St Francis de Sales gives this advice: 'The best way is a silence that is gentle and without malice. However little one says, pride always comes into it and one says things that plunge the heart into grief for a whole day after.'

So often we hear the 'if only's', if only I hadn't said such a thing, if only ... when it is too late to take it back.

Speech is such a wonderful God given gift – the main instrument through which we can communicate with each other. When one is caught up in any sort of problem or suffering the greatest healing is to be able to talk to somebody, to unburden and share with another halves the problem.

The good that we can do with this gift is endless. We can encourage and lift people through a few kind words of consolation and compassion. All the 'helpline' services, for example, are based primarily on this fact. If we could always remember the power which we hold to either lift up or tear down with our tongues, we would, I feel sure take more care with our use of them.

Lord, just for today, help us to hold back the hurtful word and unkindly remark.

Prevent us from pushing another behind a wall of loneliness and despair in an effort to keep further hurt away from them, because of our spreading scandal.

We cannot promise to change, but we can try, just for today!

MISSING THE POINT

In a lovely verse from *The Koran* we are told: 'The faith of none of you is perfect until he wishes for the other what he wishes for himself!'

Christianity is not about a private matter between myself and God. It is rather about God, myself and others. If I am just looking after my own little spot – ensuring that I get in through the gates of Heaven, regardless of what happens to others – then I am missing the point.

At any homecoming the parents will want all the family members to come, not just some. We have many examples in the Gospels of how Christ wants to gather all his flock and bring them home; in his story of the Prodigal Son, the 'black sheep' of the family receives a mighty welcome – not because the father thinks more of him, but because he was almost lost. Again, we have the example of Christ, the Good Shepherd, leaving the 99 to go off in search of the one lost sheep.

God created each member of the human family. We are His sons and daughters. Each unique and special in His eyes. He asks us to share one another's burdens, the weak must help the strong and be gentle with them. As St Paul reminds us, He has given us authority to 'lift up' not to 'tear down' each other. If we reach out with Christ's love and compassion, then our brothers and sisters will want to follow the model of Jesus which we represent.

I believe that when we arrive at the Gates of Heaven that God will ask us, 'how many of your brothers and sisters did you bring with you?'

SUICIDE

A pain too deep for sorrow too strong for tears

I read in the paper that they were looking for you. They had found your car by the river and now they were searching. I feel a kind of hopelessness that this should have happened in our midst. Did I know you? Were you, perhaps, the person next to me on the bus this morning? I thought you looked a little anxious, but I didn't bother to speak to you, I was too caught up with my own thoughts and preoccupations.

Or perhaps you were behind me in the supermarket queue, with the screaming demanding child. Why didn't I offer some help instead of just feeling irritated with the noise.

Were you the friend who has been telephoning me a lot lately, did I fail to listen to what you were not saying?

With the demands of modern living weighing heavily on the shoulders of all of us, we sometimes fail to take the time to lend a listening ear or offer a helping hand to those in need.

As society has become more sophisticated the walls that we build around us to obtain more privacy, all too often isolate us so that the loving supportive community life which people in Third World countries enjoy, is no longer the norm in our western countries. We are very impoverished by this – Mother Teresa says that the poverty of loneliness and lack of love in our western society is far worse than the material poverty in her country.

One of the greatest sufferings is the pain of loneliness, to help alleviate this pain in others we have to give of ourselves. It is said that the greatest gift we can give to another is the gift of our time – time to listen to another's pain, to encourage and lift them up when they are low. Very often the people who are hardest to love, who are sending out the negative signals through being nasty, irritable, etc., are the people who most need love and care. The aggressive retort is often only a means of testing the assurance of our love!

♥

Do all the good that you can
To all the people that you can
In all the places that you can
At all the times that you can
In all the ways that you can.

St John of God

LOVE IS A BEAUTIFUL WORD, BUT THE DEED IS MORE BEAUTIFUL STILL

(ST AUGUSTINE)

My friend Joan is all heart. She just bubbles over with love and kindness. In her goodness and generosity she often ends up trying to achieve the impossible, in a bid to be all things to all people – her heart ruling her head.

Some years ago when I had a major crisis, someone in the family had had an accident – the first person I thought of contacting was Joan. She seemed to be there within minutes, taking control of the situation with her caring and loving compassion. When the crisis was over I asked her how she had managed to get to my house so quickly, as she lives on the other side of town.

'Oh!' she said, 'I was very bold, I think I crashed all the red lights!'

Joan is the Peter in my life – that 'rock' on which Christ built his Church. The fisherman with the big heart, sometimes made some bad blunders in his attempts at loving his Master. We see him often 'putting his two feet into it', so to speak. He staunchly proclaims 'I am ready to die for you', but before the cock crows he will deny Christ three times! Then, full to the brim with remorse, he weeps bitterly at his human weakness.

A lovely legend tells us that on one occasion when St Peter was fleeing from Rome, when the Christians were undergoing

23

persecution and death, St Peter met Christ and asked Him: *'Domine, quo vadis?'* (Lord, where are you going?)

Christ replied, 'To Rome to be crucified a second time.'

Whereupon St Peter turned about and went back to Rome, where he was crucified, but refused to die in the same position as Christ – he was crucified upside down!

When Christ was choosing the person to lead his Church, the crucial question he asked Peter was: 'Do you love me more than these others do?' Love was the kernel, the 'trademark' of the man to whom he would entrust his lambs and his sheep: the little ones, the sick ones, the ones who will keep making blunders – the man with the heart full of love and compassion would understand, would know how to encourage them to try again, and again.

So thank you Joan for being the living icon of St Peter in my life.

GIFT OF KINDNESS

'She was the kindest soul ... All heart ... Generous to a fault ... Always there when someone needed a helping hand, nothing was too much trouble, and nobody ever heard about it ... She will be a great loss ...'

The above comments, overheard at a funeral jolted me into a realisation of the crucial role that kind and compassionate people play in our lives and in our world. All too often, it is only when a dear friend or someone we hold in very high esteem, has died, that we begin to appreciate that the quality that endeared them to us, most of all, was their kindness.

The gentle, kindly people often go unnoticed and unheralded, because our age is so geared towards success and achievement. We don't give points for kindness, compassion and consideration – more's the pity! The old people had a saying: 'Be good, sweet child, and let who will be clever.'

In the last century Charles Dickens, who had a passionate sympathy for the poor and oppressed and a hatred of all hypocrisy, created such kindly characters as Mr Pickwick, Mr Micawber and Betsey Trotwood in his novels. These much loved characters – all of whom were the epitome of loving-kindness – were the people who made life bearable and endurable for the pathetically poor and the victims of injustice and oppression. Everybody loved these characters, as everybody loves genuinely kind people – they provide the much needed balance/compensation for the cruelty, brashness and selfishness of others.

Kindness resembles Christ most of all, we are told. It is His love in action in the world. A kind person is quick to excuse the faults and failings of others and we are all in need of this understanding and caring.

I recently heard that a large commercial organisation were sending their staff on a course to learn what in effect amounted to courtesy and kindness towards customers! But kindness is essentially a matter of the heart. It is an inner attitude of self-lessness and self-forgetfulness.

In the Sermon on the Mount, Christ asked us to adopt the attitude of kindness. It is only by imitating His mind and heart that we can extend kindness and compassion to people who show no appreciation and who are perhaps nasty and aggressive towards us. For love is not brushed aside by insults or rudeness. As St John of the Cross says: 'Where there is no love, put love and you will draw love out'.

If we really wanted to make this a better world we would change the structures and put the qualities of kindness and compassion in place of power and success. We would award medals for kindness and like Charles Dickens we would really applaud and appreciate the generous and warm-hearted people for the richness and quality they bring to our lives and our world.

TAKE TIME TO BE KIND

No burden is too heavy
No grief too hard to bear
When there is someone kind to care.

Take time to spread a little kindness every day and help restore the balance between right and wrong in the world. For kindness is the nobility of mankind – the instinct which is the noblest part of ourselves – the part which resembles the image of God. Kindness is of the heart and springs from the warmth and gentleness of a heart concerned for the welfare of others.

The people we like most are those who are kind, for it has an infectious quality which attracts, consoles and gives us peace. Kindness excuses, makes allowances and is non-judgmental. We are all in need of kindness and the knowledge of this should keep us in touch of our need to be kind to each other. The love of our neighbour in the fullest sense simply means being able to say, 'What are you going through?' says Simone Weil.

Kindness reaches out to help and rescue, even when it hurts. It is the imitation of God's mercy, gentleness and goodness. It is treating others as we would like them to treat us.

WHAT CAN I DO?

What can I do for another today?
I will watch out for the one who needs help and care.
I will be careful not to cause any hurt to another.
I will be specially kind to the one whom I find it hardest to be
    kind to.
I will try not to be selfish.
I will try to make life full of sunshine for those I meet.
Lord, you know me better than I know myself. You know that

even though I will sincerely try to carry out these good intentions that I will fail and fail miserably. It was the same with Peter, wasn't it? He was always promising you the moon, and then coming back full of remorse when he failed. But you always took him back, you understood his weaknesses, you encouraged him to keep trying, that's the most important thing – to sincerely try. In the end, of course, Peter with the help of your Holy Spirit did succeed.

Maybe I will too.

Christ has no body now on earth but yours;
No hands but yours, no feet but yours:
Yours are the eyes through which His love looks out to the world;
Yours are the feet with which He goes about doing good;
Yours are the hands with which He blesses men now.

St Teresa of Avila

To be Sensitive is to ...

'You are far too sensitive,' he was told, 'you will have to toughen up if you hope to stay in this job!' We live in a world which doesn't applaud sensitivity in a person – toughness and ruthlessness are encouraged instead. Yet, where would we be without the sensitive people – the people who listen deeply enough to hear the pain and suffering of others.

To be sensitive means to care, to appreciate and to love – to explore deeply the cry of humanity, the 'tears' of things.

A young man wrote about how deeply he felt the pain of bereavement. 'My heart was black with grief. Whatever I looked upon had the air of death. My native place was a prison-house and my home had a strange unhappiness. The things we had done together became sheer torment. I had no delight but in tears, for tears had taken the place my friend had held in the love of my heart.'

This young man was sensitive and caring, the love which he felt for his friend eventually led him to seek out the author and creator of love Himself. We come to God through each other. The more sensitive and caring we are towards our fellow human beings the closer we come to God.

Many years later this young man wrote: 'You have made us for Yourself O Lord and our hearts are restless until they rest in You.' He was St Augustine of Hippo.

WE ARE OUR BROTHER'S KEEPER

It is a common fallacy to believe that loneliness is a problem which only affects the elderly and house-bound. While our elderly are certainly amongst those most affected, however, all age groups suffer; young children, teenagers, young mothers, the middle-aged married people as well as single people. Neither is this problem confined to any sector of society – money does not protect one.

During the past 30 years in Ireland we have witnessed the growth of a consumer society, where the emphasis lies in acquiring the luxuries which money can buy. We have become very independent, we don't need people any more. The tradition of just 'dropping in' to visit people has practically stopped. We feel that we need to telephone first or that they may be busy watching television and not welcome the intrusion. The old tradition of 'neighbourliness' has practically come to an end.

The increase of violence and crime which, incidentally, is mostly about acquiring more money for luxuries or for drugs, by fair means or foul, means that we have become suspicious of strangers and rarely invite them into their homes. The elderly have, in many cases, retreated behind locked doors, or into full-time care. The hurt and fear caused by the increase in crime is further alienating people.

In the 1960s, the song *The Streets of London* told us about the plight of the lonely in a metropolis like London; where a person could become totally isolated in a society that didn't care! Where someone could spend hours 'looking at the world over the rim of his teacup' and then wander home 'lonely and alone'. Where a poor old lady went about 'carrying her home in two carrier bags'. We pitied these people but felt that this couldn't happen here. Well, look at the number of lonely people wandering about the streets of our major cities – the 'walking dead,' expressionless people, hurt and unloved. We have people of all ages 'sleeping rough' because for one reason or another they have become alienated from society and don't 'fit in'. Between four and five thousand people are homeless in Ireland today.

Materialism encourages us to be independent – we can manage on our own, we don't need other people. Then something – like a major disaster – brings home to us how dependant we are on each other. The world is a community, the human family, dependant upon each other for our very survival. The community is made up of young and old, sick and able-bodied. At some stage in our lives we find that we become dependant on the love, care and generosity of others, so it is not true that we can live independently of each other.

Loneliness can lead to apathy, self-neglect and eventually loss of self-respect. It can lead to depression, despair and even suicide. It can be difficult to discern the 'face' of loneliness in our midst. Pride prevents people from telling us that they are lonely, so we have to take time to look behind the 'masks'.

But how does one tackle the problem? Awareness is the first step, the next move is action – let's care enough to act! Groups of people like the Samaritans do wonderful work, but it is not enough to leave it to the few. We can all contribute in some way; a smile, a kind word – the most precious gift we can give to another is the gift of our time; time to be there for somebody who needs someone to listen. By reaching out to others, letting them become part of our lives we find that we help ourselves. If you are feeling lonely, deciding to do something about it is to overcome the biggest hurdle.

> *What Europe needs today is a soul.*
> COMMISSIONER JACQUES DELORS

♥

HEART OF THE HOSPITAL WARD

Mary acted as mother to the little group of women in the ward. She was a big warm-hearted gentle person, with a lovely open smile and dancing eyes. She had been in the ward longer than anybody and took it on herself to make each newcomer feel welcome and at home. 'I remember how frightened and anxious I felt when I came here first,' she explained, and wanted to prevent others from going through that pain.

Mary's kindness managed to transform a sterile hospital ward into a place of warmth and love. She was an ardent reader and there were always three or four books on her locker. 'Reading keeps me alert, since I was a very small child I have been able to escape into different worlds through my books, and God has been very good, I still don't even need reading glasses at 87 years of age,' she told me.

Mary never married, her parents were long since dead and her only brother had died tragically some years ago, so Mary was all alone in the world now. 'That is why I can't go home anymore,' she explained sadly, 'there is nobody to look after me now that I am bedridden.'

But Mary never dwelled on her own problems, she was too busy thinking of the needs of others.

At three o'clock every day Mary said the Rosary, and as the other women responded they took strength and comfort from her strong firm faith. Sometimes at night when all the visitors had gone she would read aloud to them soothing them off to sleep.

At visiting times she would explain how poor Nora had a very bad night, tossing and turning, worrying about her family. How the lady in the corner, whose house had been broken into was terrified of living alone again Mary's soothing assurance helped them to come through their traumas and she gave them the courage to face life again. She saw the best in everybody and never spoke about their faults.

One day I arrived to find an air of sadness in the ward – Mary had been shifted, the heart had gone from the ward! The nurse explained that they needed the bed for a more critical patient and had to move Mary to the older part of the hospital which was reserved for long-term patients.

I didn't notice her at first, she seemed somehow lost in the vastness of the large old ward. She was lying down amongst the blankets, a shadow of her former self. For the first time, there was no smile and my heart sank. 'This is the beginning of the end for me,' she said sadly, 'you see, everybody else here is a little bit senile, and I will become like that now as well because I won't have anybody to talk to.'

I tried to give her some assurances, but we both knew that she was right! She didn't feel like reading anymore, she just wasn't feeling up to it. Lord, I prayed, why does this have to happen to someone so helpless and vulnerable?

Just two weeks later I received a phone call to say that Mary had died peacefully in her sleep. Her worst fears hadn't been realised after all! The Great Physician Himself had intervened and taken Mary to a better home.

LIFT SOMEONE UP!

John belongs to an association for people who suffer from an addiction. He is full to the brim with love, kindness and compassion. All of his free time is spent helping those who suffer from the addiction which he himself was once caught up in. He is quick to tell you that he is not cured, the compulsion will always be there, but with God's help he has managed to steer clear of it now for some 12 years.

He knows the pain involved in being 'in hell', which is why he will travel any distance at any hour of the night to help someone caught up in the same agony. If he has managed to lighten the burden, to 'lift-up' someone, then it has been a good day for John. He is totally convinced that his 'cure' did not come about through his own efforts, it was the Lord's intervention – that is why his time and effort is dedicated to freeing people from the slavery of an addiction.

♥

BEACON OF HOPE

There's a certain magic about Christmas. The excitement, the glitter, the tinsel, the carol-singing and the general air of goodwill as people rush about buying presents, posting Christmas cards, meeting friends. It's impossible not to be caught up in the excitement – in the air of celebration – as the song says 'Love, changes everything'. This is what is happening, it is all about the outpouring of love, the thinking of and caring for others.

It is visible in the general sense of giving, of goodwill and good humour, as people jostle to buy gifts, joining long queues in post offices and shops and taking time and effort to choose just the right present for loved ones. What it all adds up to is the fact that we are happiest forgetting ourselves and reaching out to others – the essence of love, putting others' needs before our own.

But this can be the loneliest and most difficult time of the entire year for some people. It is the time, for instance, when the highest suicide figures are recorded.

Billy, a widower, told me that he hates Christmas nowadays. There was a time when he absolutely loved it, but that was when his children were young and the house was full of the joy and expectation that children bring. He lives alone now. His children are all abroad, so he finds it very lonely and just wants to see the back of it!

FOR NAN, CHRISTMAS IS A NIGHTMARE! From the time her husband collects his pay packet a few days before Christmas until he is back at work again after the New Year, the family live in dread of his alcoholic outbursts of temper and rage.

'He just goes on one long binge,' said Nan. 'It's a miserable time for the family, we count the days until he has to sober up to get back to work again.'

The priests, hospital staffs, members of the Vincent de Paul Society, Samaritans, the gardaí and social workers, all work extremely hard both in preparation for and throughout the Christmas season. They lead the way in ensuring that the season of goodwill is experienced by the poor and the marginalised in our midst.

Jesus entered this world through the door of poverty and marginalisation and yet the joy and love which he brought to our world on that first Christmas still shines forth. It is a beacon of hope, which permeates every corner and crevice of our universe – which will never cease to shine.

It is not the glitter or the tinsel or the bright lights which give Christmas its magic – it is the love of the little Christ child!

JEAN VANIER – FOUNDER OF L'ARCHE

A living witness of the compassionate face of Christ's love present to some of His most precious, vulnerable people today, is that humble champion of the mentally handicapped – Jean Vanier, Founder of L'Arche.

My encounter with this softly-spoken, 'gentle-giant' took place during one of his visits to this country where a number of L'Arche communities and L'Arche workshops exist, in Kilkenny, Dublin and Cork.

A person of tremendous charisma, when he speaks his message touches the hearts of his listeners. It is not difficult to understand, it is just the simple Gospel message of love.

He explains that the story of L'Arche began with the Gospel story – 'this is where it has its roots'. It grew out of the searching of a young man who wanted to follow Jesus and discovered that He is hidden in the weak, the poor and the marginalised people. It was, he says, born from a desire to help and recognise the value and the contribution which handicapped people make to our society and our world.

'It grew because there is something true about it and the truth is that people with handicaps reveal to us who we are. They reveal to us our beauty, but they also reveal to us our brokenness ...'

It was founded, very simply, on the words of Jesus when He said: when you give a meal don't invite the members of your own family, or your friends, or your rich neighbours. If you do, maybe it is just so that you will be invited back. So when you give a banquet invite the lame, the poor, the crippled and the blind and you will be blessed. 'This is the foundation of L'Arche, to eat with the poor, and eating is simply to enter into communion with them and become their friends'.

French/Canadian by birth, Jean grew up in what he describes as 'a good Catholic family'. One of five children, his eldest brother became a Trappist monk, his sister a doctor, and another brother an artist. Both his parents had a strong influence on him; his mother, whom he describes as a very spiritual and prayerful person, and his father, who later became Governor General of Canada.

Like many young people, growing up he wasn't overly interested in religion and planned a career in the navy, which he entered having left school.

It was his lifelong friend and co-founder of L'Arche, Dominican priest, Pere Thomas, who influenced his decision to leave the navy, at the age of twenty-one in order to study philosophy. He had gradually become more interested in the spiritual and found, for example, that when his brother officers were going dancing, he was going to church! He received a Doctorate in Philosophy and taught at the University of Toronto.

His first introduction to mentally handicapped people occurred when Fr Thomas invited him to visit the home for mentally handicapped people, where he was chaplain. On that occasion Jean admits that he felt embarrassed, not knowing how to communicate with them. 'Until that time I knew nothing about people with handicaps. I knew about war ships, about philosophy, but until then I had always been amongst those who had succeeded in life. I started visiting psychiatric hospitals and found a whole world of those who had lost and not won!'

Initially, he invited two men with disabilities to come to live with him, close to Fr Thomas' house – and this was the beginning of L'Arche! 'When we begin to communicate and enter into the world of people with handicaps it is we who receive – it is we, ourselves, who become healed,' he says. 'It's a two-way reality, as we welcome those that frequently society rejects, or whom we reject, we become healed and find inner liberation and peace – find Jesus!'

For the founder of L'Arche, the whole meaning of Church is that we become the forgiving, loving, confirming Presence of Jesus for each other. 'Our world is lost in the sense that people don't know which way to go. God's presence is being denied and yet there is incredible thirst for it!'

He would urge people generally to slow down, to risk

meeting people – particularly those who are different – in their weakness and in their vulnerability. 'If we move out and enter into communion and communication with people who are different we will be on the road to healing and wholeness'.

Many thousands of young people throughout the world today see L'Arche as a place of vocation, a place where they are called by Jesus to live and work. Some just spend a year or two, while an ever increasing number are making a lifelong commitment to this ecumenical community.

At present Jean spends six months of the year living at his first community in Trosly in France. The other six months are spent visiting communities and helping set up new places of hope and love in a world where for many there is no hope!

The most striking quality about Jean Vanier – apart from his great height and aristocratic bearing – is his smile. He has an amazing smile, which radiates warmth and expresses a mammoth depth of peace and compassion. It is the outward expression of the caring kindness and love at the heart of this champion of the needy!

Only those who have suffered have beautiful faces.

JEAN VANIER

L'ARCHE COMMUNITIES

L'Arche Communities are places where people with a mental handicap live and work together in an atmosphere of mutual giving, love and respect, with those society calls 'normal'. They provide a family atmosphere within small houses which are well integrated into the local district. L'Arche workshops provide different kinds of work where each person can find fulfilment and opportunity for growth.

People with a mental handicap are the heart of these communities. Many come from institutions, and those without family or friends have first priority. Founded in 1964, at Trosly France, L'Arche today has over a hundred communities spread throughout thirty countries worldwide.

The aim of L'Arche is to create communities which welcome people with mental handicap. L'Arche seeks to respond to the distress of those who are too often rejected, and to give them a valid place in the community.

'The person with a mental handicap only asks for the essential. Meanwhile the world doesn't want the essential; we want riches and power. But our people seek the essential. They want to be loved.'

THANK YOU

Thank you for understanding my faltering step and unsteady hand.

Thank you for realising that my ears must strain to catch the things you say.

Thank you for seeming to know that my eyes are dim and my memory slow.

Thank you for looking away when the soup spilled today.

Thank you for stopping to chat with your cheerful smile and friendly way.

Thank you for not reminding me that I had told that story twice today.

Thank you for listening as I rambled back amidst memories of yesterday.

Thank you for letting me know that I'm loved, respected and not alone.

Thank you for realising that I'm at a loss to find the strength to carry the Cross.

Thank you for easing the days on my journey home in loving and caring ways.

Thank you most of all just for being my friend.

HOPE

HAPPINESS IS ....

What is happiness? What is this elusive something that we all try so hard to find and hold on to? At different stages of our lives we put certain connotations on what it is and how it can be achieved. Very often, only to find that when we actually grasp what we have perceived it to be, we are disappointed or disillusioned. And so, our search continues in ever differing directions.

As a child, I thought that the ultimate happiness would be to have enough money to buy dozens of bars of chocolate. When I got to the stage of being able to buy as much chocolate as I wanted, I realised that this type of over-indulgence would not make me happy at all.

Young people today are encouraged to believe that pleasure seeking, and all that that entails, is the ultimate goal whereby they will find happiness. Position and power are also seen as roads to happiness, but over and above all, money is looked upon as the ultimate happiness, by those who believe that luxuries and all the things that money can buy, bring happiness! Consequently, there are a large number of very miserable, rich people in this world.

Money has very little to do with happiness. Certainly in cases of extreme poverty it is very necessary to help relieve hardship, but not as an end in itself.

The happiest people I know are the people who are generous and caring, whose lives revolve around looking after others. Like the mother of a very large family I know, who has had a great deal of suffering and hardship in her life, but she is too caught up in the business of caring and looking after her family, her neighbours and friends, to allow herself indulge in any type of self-pity. 'Health is wealth' is her motto.

We do catch fleeting glimpses of joy and happiness in the ordinary everyday strivings; in companionship, friendships and the little serendipities of life – in beauty, music, art, the wonder of nature and the innate goodness of people, in contentment and peace.

But we can never hope to find complete happiness this side of Heaven – this elusive something belongs to our final home!

You have made us for Yourself, O Lord
And our hearts are restless, until they rest in You.

St Augustine

LET GO, AND LET GOD

It is easy to praise and thank God when things are going well – when the sun is shining in our lives – but quite a different matter when we meet with life's hurts and disappointments. When everything is going well for us, we tend to believe that we have somehow gained God's favour and approval, and that He is really pleased with us.

Whereas, when we meet the difficulties, disappointments and tragedies in life, we can feel that God has somehow let us down, or even turned His back on us altogether. One often hears the comment: 'How could God let this happen', or 'What did I do to deserve this?' That was the thinking of the people in the Old Testament. When some misfortune befell them they saw this as a sign that they had somehow or other incurred the wrath of God – that he was displeased with them.

With the coming of Christ, we learned that God was love, full to the brim with loving-kindness, and that He is in fact closest to the broken-hearted people. However, it can be very hard to continue to believe in His goodness during our most difficult times. But this is the real test of faith – to continue to walk, or just stumble along with hope and trust, through the 'dark' times, when the light is not visible.

Some of the saints, St John of the Cross in particular, wrote about this 'Dark Night of the Soul', a period in our lives when we feel deprived of God's presence, at a time of great suffering and trauma when we need Him most of all. It was during this period in his life that St John of the Cross wrote some of his most beautiful poetry.

Often we see that 'the darkest hour is always before the dawn' – that new life often emerges out of pain and suffering. There is always light at the end of the tunnel and Christ has, in fact, assured us that He is there carrying us through our darkest times!

Faith means 'letting go, and letting God' – trusting blindly in His goodness and mercy to carry us when we are unable to carry ourselves!

♥

THE HUMAN TOUCH

The gift of encouragement is one of the greatest gifts of all – to lift up someone who is down, who has lost heart. As a drooping plant recovers instantly when we water it, so do our drooping spirits need encouragement so that we can feel that we are valuable and have something to contribute.

Have you ever noticed how someone with shoulders bent, head drooped and eyes dull from disillusionment, pain or discouragement will react when given a few kind words of encouragement. There are many people walking about for whom life has lost its purpose. As Christians we have a duty towards each other. Christ was always offering encouragement to those who needed it. Look at all the stories in the Bible – He was constantly lifting up those who needed encouragement, the sinners and the outcasts of society. Before he corrected them he gave them back their dignity – he reminded them that they were valuable and special in the eyes of God.

Isn't it wonderful to have the power to be able to help someone to hold their heads high again, to put a smile back on the face of the person who has almost forgotten how to smile. To help put a spring back into their step and to let them see that they are valuable and needed!

Every human being is valuable and special in the eyes of God – we are only reminding them of this fact through the word of encouragement! To encourage others literally means to put God into them – to be 'an encourager' is to preach the Gospel, to give new life.

EVERY NEW DAY IS ...

The first buds of spring have already appeared. They bravely shoot through in spite of all sorts of adverse weather conditions. They lift our hearts with the assurance that even though all may seem grey, cold and dismal in our January world, these tiny buds appear full of hope and expectation.

Gerald Manly Hopkins wrote 'The world is charged with the grandeur of God'. God is always speaking to us through the wonder of nature. Just as surely as the death and decay of autumn give way to rebirth in the spring, so it is with our lives. We experience the pain and suffering of different 'deaths' going through life – bereavement, illness, separation from loved ones and many others – but Christ assures us that He is there with us. He has been through all these experiences. Every new day is a new opportunity filled with hope and promise – a fresh canvas with which to begin again!

THE DAFFODILS

I wandered lonely as a cloud
That floats on high o'er vales and hills
When all at once I saw a crowd,
A host of golden daffodils;
Beside the lake, beneath the trees,
Fluttering and dancing in the breeze.
Continuous as the stars that shine
And twinkle on the Milky Way,
They stretch'd in never-ending line
Along the margin of a bay;
Ten thousand saw I at a glance
Tossing their heads in sprightly dance.

The waves beside them danced, but they
Out-did the sparkling waves in glee.
A poet could not but be gay
In such a jocund company!
I gazed – and gazed – but little thought
What wealth the show to me had brought:

For oft, when on my couch I lie
In vacant or in pensive mood,
They flash upon that inward eye
Which is the bliss of solitude;
And then my heart with pleasure fills,
And dances with the daffodils.

WILLIAM WORDSWORTH

OPEN YOUR EYES

'I'm stuck, like a dope, to a thing called hope ...'

These words from the song in *South Pacific*, express, albeit in a flippant way, the strongest message of the Christian faith.

In our darkest moments hope can mean the difference, literally, between life and death. It can make us see this world as a challenge when the clouds of darkness seem to engulf us. Hope is the chink of sunlight which is never extinguished, which brushes away all fear.

Sadness and suffering are part of life, nobody escapes, but intertwined with the grief and the pain are the miracles, the joys the everyday serendipities, if our eyes are open to see them.

A PHILOSOPHY FOR LIFE

GOD IS GOOD he told them when sorrow and suffering visited their home.

GOD IS GOOD he reminded them when happiness and joy reigned free once again.

GOD IS GOOD he repeated, through smudged tears, as each one left to find their own way in the world.

Many years after his passing they reflected that his hope-filled 'gem' contained a whole philosophy for living.

Because GOD IS GOOD, full to the very brim with love, generosity, compassion and kindness, nothing in this world could ever daunt them, in this sure knowledge that – GOD IS GOOD!

ALL THAT IS GOOD

Are you feeling depressed and low, bowed down by too many worries and too much pressure? Perhaps you are trying to recover from the death of a loved one and feel that life has very little purpose for you. The cares and crosses of life can enslave us, sap our energy and steal our joy. But God is always encouraging us to meet Him and to see His hand and His love in all the good and uplifting things.

Go out into the countryside and He will show you His majesty and might in the wonder of His mountains. The power of His strength in His mighty ocean. Experience His gentleness in the sweet song of the birds and the soft breeze. He will show you that His good fresh air will act as a sedative to rest and soothe you. Look at the awesome beauty of the sunset. Just rest awhile and allow yourself time to reflect and wonder. He calls out to us, through the beauty of nature, to really meet His warm heart and warm embrace and find renewed strength and hope to carry on. When Christ said 'Come to me all of you who are weary from carrying heavy burdens and I will give you rest' – He meant what He said, and we must expect nothing less of Him, He did not mean it in the abstract!

I SEE HIS BLOOD UPON THE ROSE

I see His blood upon the rose
And in the stars the glory of His eyes
His body gleams amid eternal snows
His tears fall from the skies.

I see His face in every flower
The thunder and the singing of the birds

Are but His voice; and carven by His power
Rocks are His written words.

All pathways by His feet are worn
His strong heart stirs the ever-beating sea
His crown of thorns is twined by every thorn
His cross is every tree.

JOSEPH MARY PLUNKETT

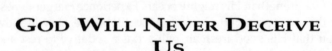

GOD WILL NEVER DECEIVE US

Love must be completely sincere and truthful, we are told in the Scriptures. However, people may not read God's Word in the Scriptures, but they will see how we lead our lives and the example which our lives give may be the only doorway through which people will seek to find the image of God.

The preacher held the people spellbound, they hung on to every word which came out of his mouth. It wasn't the eloquence of his speech or the intellectual content of what he spoke about – it was the fact that he put his whole heart and soul into every word. He was speaking from the heart – the pure, simple, truth and sincerity of his words touched their hearts.

He told them that they had no need to worry, sure wasn't God looking after all of us, and he assured them that 'God would never "deceive" us'. Looking at his lovely open smile they knew for certain that he would never deceive them and as he was speaking for God then neither would God!

People who are open, honest, loving and trusting are very vulnerable because they do not use the masks and the barriers which most of us adopt to protect us from the slights and the hurts in life. Christ does not use any barriers – His heart is continually open and loving, that is why he suffered so much inner pain and it is why He is so understanding and compassionate towards us. It is why He tells us that unless we become like little children, loving, trusting without guile or malice, we cannot enter the Kingdom of Heaven.

♥

THE GREAT FATHER

'There's a wideness in God's mercy like the wideness of the
    sea:
There's a kindness in His justice, which is more than liberty.

There is no place where Earth's sorrows are more felt than up
    in Heaven.
There is no place where Earth's failings have such kind judge-
    ment given.

For the love of God is broader than the measure of man's
    mind,
And the heart of the eternal is most wonderfully kind.

But we make His love too narrow by false limits of our own:
And we magnify His strictness with a zeal He will not own.

If our love were but more simple, we should take Him at His
    word,
And our lives would be all sunshine in the sweetness of Our
    Lord.

FR F. W. FABER

♥

49

SIMPLE MESSAGE

The Christian message is not difficult or complicated, it is very simple. God wishes us to call Him 'Abba' which means Father and wants us to have a child-like trust in Him.

When Christ was preaching to the people He used simple stories from everyday life – called parables – in order to get His message across to them. Let's take an example of how He would wish us to live with a child-like trust in Him:

Consider this world as a large garden, bathed in sunshine. People live happily in this garden, caring and sharing each others' joy and sorrows. Christ is there at the centre in the role of a loving parent. He wants us to come to Him for guidance and direction with our lives, for healing when we are experiencing pain and suffering. He will teach us how to love as He loves us and asks that we turn to Him constantly and trust Him totally.

There is one corner of the garden however which is dark and gloomy. He cautions us not to enter that area because if we do we will cut ourselves off from the light of His love. In order to go into this part of the garden we have to turn our backs on Him first. He cannot go in after us.

He has given us free will to make our own choices. However, because He continues to love us in spite of what we do when and if we do turn back He is there waiting to carry us back in His arms into the warmth and sunshine of His love again.

ALWAYS REASON FOR HOPE

An old Chinese proverb says: 'If you only have two pennies, buy a loaf of bread with one – and a flower with the other.'

These wise words emphasise the importance and necessity of the nourishment of Hope and Joy which our human spirits crave and continually yearn for. We are more than mere flesh and blood!

On a visit to Moscow I was struck by the drabness of the seemingly endless rows of uniform brown/grey apartment blocks – the homes of thousands of Muscovites. Many had broken window panes and shabby, starkly drawn, pieces of material acting as a means of ensuring privacy from the outside world. What was most disconcerting about the whole scene was the lack of colour. There were no flowers, not a plant or even a vase of flowers on any of the window sills.

And yet, the Russian people love flowers and have a long tradition of using them to express both joy and sorrow. Our guide, for example, pointed out that the magnificent St Basil's Cathedral in Red Square was designed 'like a beautiful flower to give thanks to God for freeing us from the oppression of a Tartar's yoke'.

It appeared that the lack of any visible display of flowers in the apartment windows said a great deal about the sense of hopelessness and apathy that resulted from a system that sought to crush and dominate the spirit of the people.

One of the most disturbing headlines ever to appear in a newspaper was one that screamed: 'Abandon Hope'.

The only place where hope is ever abandoned is, as the poet Dante pointed out in his immortal phrase, over the Gates of Hell – 'Abandon all hope, ye who enter here!'

Hope is the central theme of the whole Christian message. There is always, always reason for hope. This is the whole kernel of our faith. 'Do not be afraid, little flock, I have overcome the world'.

COURAGE

THE HERO OF THE LEPERS OF MOLOKOI

Every picture tells a story. The portrait of the zealous young priest with the strong determined face, setting out on his arduous and lonely missionary journey, certainly inspired admiration and respect. But it was the second picture of the poor disfigured creature, face and body horribly distorted and wasted by a cruel disease, that touched the hearts of an often indifferent world.

This figure which, for love of the poorest of the poor, had taken on in his own body their cry of anguished pain, caused the world to stop and say, through the words of Ghandi: 'the world of politics and of the press knows few heroes comparable to Fr Damien of Molokai. It would be very worthwhile to discover the source inspiring so much heroism!'

As a child I remember being fascinated by the story of Fr Damien, the priest, who went to the island of Molokai to minister and care for the poor – discarded and set aside by society.

Fully aware of the perilous nature of the mission he was undertaking, Damien was determined to be Christ's love in action for those abandoned and alienated people. Having spent eleven years caring and nurturing them, one morning at Mass he made the inevitable announcement 'And we lepers' – he, himself had contracted the dreaded disease and was now truly one of them!

This 'hero' of the leper colony of Molokai was beatified by Pope John Paul II in 1995. He was born Joseph de Veuster, at Tremelo in Belgium on 3 January 1840, the second son of a large family, whose father was a farm merchant. When his oldest brother entered the Congregation of the Sacred Hearts to become a priest, his father planned that his second son should take charge of the family business. However, Joseph decided that he, too, wished to join the priesthood and in 1859 entered the novitiate at Louvain, in the same house as his brother. There he took his name in religion – Damien. He set forth as a missionary for the Hawaiian Islands, even before his Ordination, at the age of 24. His brother, who was to have gone, had been taken ill, so Damien sought and received permission to go in his place. He arrived in Honolulu on 19 March 1864 and was ordained to the priesthood the following 21 May.

In an effort to stop the spread of the dreaded disease of leprosy, which was rife in the Hawaiian Islands, the Government decided to deport all those infected to the island of Molokai. The Congregation of the Sacred Hearts, Fr Damien's Order, who had undertaken the Catholic Church's missionary effort in that whole area of Oceania, became very concerned for the abandoned 'lepers'. The bishop, Louis Maigret, SSCC, did not want to send anyone 'under obedience', knowing that such a mission meant certain death, as the disease of leprosy was highly contagious with no known cure. However, four members of the Congregation volunteered to go to the aid of the lepers and Fr Damien was the first to leave on 10 May 1873.

The conditions he found on the island were appalling, with the 'lepers' living in a terrible state of hunger, squalor and misery without any type of medical aid. Noted for his stubborn determination, the young priest set about nursing and caring for all the needs of the inhabitants; dressing their sores with his own hands, building their coffins and burying their dead. His tremendous compassion and kindness created a sense of hope and happiness in the little colony.

As time went by Fr Damien gradually improved their living conditions. He laid a pipeline to bring fresh water to the settlement and set up a little hospital. His pioneering work became known throughout the world drawing attention to the plight of the lepers. Doctors and nurses came to the hospital he had started.

Fr Damien never left his lepers – he stayed on Molokai with them for the remainder of his life: 'I am happy and content and if I were given the choice of leaving here in order to be cured I would answer without hesitation "I'll remain here with my lepers as long as I live".' He continued his work for nearly four years after contracting the disease himself and died on 15 April 1889, at the age of 49.

For 47 years he lay buried on Molokai but in 1936 his body was disinterred and taken back to Belgium, where a state funeral was held in his memory, attended by King Leopold III, King of the Belgians.

During his lifetime, Damien had suffered the mental anguish of unjust criticism and misunderstanding from people, he had endured the painful solitude of the missionary and eventually the onslaughts of the horrible disease. It was his tremendous faith and in particular, devotion to the Eucharist which gave him the strength and courage to persevere in such difficult circumstances: 'Without the presence of our Divine Master in my small chapel, I would never be able to sustain my life united to that of the lepers of Molokai.'

Of this great future saint the writer Robert Louis Stevenson said: 'It was his part, by one striking act of martyrdom, to direct all men's eyes to this distressful country ... If ever any man brought reforms and died to bring them it was he'.

♥

IN THE LORD'S HANDS
Coping with Terminal Illness

You told me that you had a terminal illness. There was a quiet dignity about you when we met for a 'cuppa'. As I rummaged and fumbled with expressions of sympathy and remorse, you apologised for having upset me. You said that, somehow, you had got the grace to accept the inevitable.

'I am in the Lord's hands,' you said and even joked, 'sure isn't there only a loan of all of us in the world!' You were more concerned about your family and friends – they were so upset and in need of support, you felt.

Of course, you had felt anger initially, anger with God even, but you had worked through all of that now and felt a total acceptance. God was calling you to a better place.

You wanted people to treat you as normally as possible. You wanted to continue to live your life in the usual mould for as long as you could, you said. As we chatted about the ups and downs of life, I marvelled at your ability to cope so well and at your philosophical approach to your illness and your situation. 'I have just come to the realisation that there are no certainties in this world, that ultimately we have to let go of everything and everyone,' you said.

We are all conscious of this fact, but we tend to bury it at the back of our minds. It's something we don't really want to have to face, just yet. Something, like Scarlet O'Hara, we'll think about tomorrow!

But your courage and acceptance amazed me. My heart went out to you as you spoke about the sadness you felt at leaving your family, in particular. They would find it very difficult to keep going at first, you knew that, but you were convinced that God would help and take care of them for you.

You were very much in tune with the Lord. You told me that you talk to Him a lot. No, you don't say many formal prayers – they were, after all, only composed by others – you said. You just talk to Him as you would with a good friend and you are very conscious of the ways in which he speaks to you.

To a certain extent, I felt talking to you, that you had already begun to leave us. That your sights and even desires were focused on the homeward journey. You were utterly convinced that Jesus was holding your hand – you were in the tender care of His most compassionate love. My eyes brimmed with tears as you said: 'He was always closest to those who were sick and brokenhearted'.

Your childlike faith and trust was an example to me.

CHRISTIANITY IS NOT EASY

We are often reminded that 'all it takes for evil to prosper is for good men to remain silent'. The early Christians would have been very conscious and aware of the fact that they had to be prepared to stand up and declare themselves as followers of Christ, and accept the consequences – often persecution and death – which this entailed in that decadent world of the failing Roman Empire. In our age, by and large, we seem to have the mistaken idea that Christianity has more to do with complacency than courage and being prepared to stand up with the courage of our convictions.

Some years ago I remember seeing a film which has had a lasting impression on me ever since. The film was called *Never Take No for an Answer*. It told the story of a little boy who decided that the pope was the only person who could solve a particular problem for him, and so he was determined that somehow he would get a private interview with the pontiff.

We sat through several hours watching the poor little lad as he struggled with insults and rejections in his effort to achieve his goal. Everybody, it seemed, was against him. But he kept persevering and persevering, accepting each rebuff – he would turn around, dust himself down, and try again.

Eventually, of course, he got there. All the frustrations, all the pain had paid off – he had achieved his goal.

Speaking to the Corinthians [2 Cor. 4:8–10], St Paul told them of the difficulties which following Christ entailed: 'We are often troubled, but not crushed; sometimes in doubt, but never in despair; there are many enemies, but we are never without a friend; and though badly hurt at times, we are not destroyed ...' Following in Christ's footsteps in every age requires a great deal of courage and perseverance. The way will not be made easy – because to follow Christ means standing up to anything in the world which stands in the way of His law of love, kindness and compassion.

He does not ask us to walk alone. He accompanies us every step of the way. But all the difficulties, pain and suffering involved will quickly fade into insignificance in the inexpressible joy we will experience when we finally come face to face with the friend we have been faithfully following.

A Psalm of Life

Tell me not, in mournful numbers,
Life is but an empty dream! –
For the soul is dead that slumbers,
And things are not what they seem.

Life is real! Life is earnest!
And the grave is not its goal;
Dust thou art, to dust returnest,
Was not spoken to the soul.

Not enjoyment, and not sorrow,
Is our destined end or way;
But to act, that each tomorrow
Find us farther than today.

Art is long, and Time is fleeting,
And our hearts, though stout and brave,
Still, like muffled drums, are beating
Funeral marches to the grave.

In the world's broad field of battle,
In the bivouac of Life,
Be not like dumb, driven cattle!
Be a hero in the strife!

Trust no Future, howe'er pleasant!
Let the dead Past bury its dead!
Act – act in the living Present!

Heart within, and God o'er head!

Lives of great men all remind us
We can make our lives sublime,
And, departing, leave behind us,
Footprints on the sand of time;

Footprints, that perhaps another,
Sailing o'er life's solemn main,
A forlorn and shipwrecked brother,
Seeing, shall take heart again.

Let us, then, be up and doing,
With a heart for any fate;
Still achieving, still pursuing,
Learn to labour and to wait.

HENRY WADSWORTH LONGFELLOW

GOODBYES ARE ALWAYS PAINFUL

Limping back to Happiness again

There is a time of year when we remember specially those whom we have loved and had to part with – never to meet them again on this side of Heaven! Saying goodbye to someone we love is always painful – saying a final farewell, or perhaps even being denied the opportunity because of sudden death – is one of the most painful experiences in life.

When Kay's husband died suddenly, leaving her with six children, the youngest of whom was only seven, she wanted to stop living herself. Her whole life had fallen apart and she just disintegrated into what she terms 'a deep, dark abyss of despair'.

'I really do believe that there is such a thing as a broken

heart – my heart really did break with Jim's death. There was no will left in me to carry on.'

The children she feels really lost both parents for a time.

'I lived in a sort of a twilight zone, surviving on sleeping pills and just about anything that would numb the pain. I was trying to put a face on it, keeping up a front for the sake of the children – but I wasn't able emotionally to relate to them at all. All I really wanted to do was lie down and die myself.

'I couldn't wait for evening time, when I could crawl into bed and cry and cry and cry in the darkened room. I used to imagine that the whole thing was just a bad dream from which I would wake up and realise that it wasn't true. In a sense, yes, I really did at times feel that he was very close, and of course, I now believe that he really was there supporting and helping me to cope. But everything and every place reminded me of him and even the happiest memories just became instruments causing a deeper, more penetrating pain.

'I used to try to pray, but spent a great deal of time being angry with God for taking him and letting me down, as I felt he had. But I begged Him for help, asking him to lessen the awful loneliness which I felt. I constantly carried a little crucifix in the palm of my hand, just for the support!'

Her friends were the 'angels of mercy' who carried her through. Not pushing or rushing her, just gently and patiently being there for her. 'They saved my sanity really'. Gradually she began to want to live again.

'I suppose also I realised, or had come to a stage when I was able to recognise that I couldn't remain sad for ever. That it wasn't fair to those around me and I got the strength, somehow, to let my head rule my heart. I took a decision to help myself, if only for the sake of my family and friends.

'Then, the day came when I smiled again!'

One of the finest insights which we have of the sensitivity and compassion of Jesus, is at the Last Supper when He is, ever so gently, breaking the news to the Apostles, His best friends, that He has to leave them – that He is about to die.

We see how He gives them hope. He knows that they are full of sadness now but He tells them that their sadness will turn to joy because He is going to the Father and He assures them that He will do whatever they will ask for in His name.

'Love one another' He counsels them – this will be their strength and support one for the other. He tells them He will not leave them orphans – He will send His own Holy Spirit to remain with them to help them, and finally He leaves them His own peace – a peace which the world is unable to give them. His sensitivity again shines through as He says that He has much more to tell them but knows that, after the shock they have had, 'now it would be too much for you to bear.'

Jesus wept when told of His friend Lazarus' death. Listening to Him we know that our loved ones are in the tenderest, loving care and we know that He will help, comfort and reassure us as He did the Apostles, through our sorrow and raw pain.

Suffering is like a deep ocean that you cannot hope to wade through because it is too deep. All you can do is float across it using the Cross of Christ as a raft.

St Augustine

Perhaps, if we could see
The splendour of the land
To which our loved are
Called from you and me
We'd Understand.

Perhaps, if we could hear
The welcome they receive
From old familiar voices – All so dear –
We Would Not Grieve.

Perhaps, if we could know
The reason why they went

63

We'd smile – and wipe away
The tears that flow
WE'D WAIT CONTENT.

CARMEL, TALLOW

DEPRESSION

There's a grief that can't be spoken, there's a pain that goes on and on
LES MISERABLES

I noticed you sitting alone, nursing a cup between your hands. Your thin, drawn face bore a haunted faraway expression, your suffering was almost tangible.

I remember the happy smiling schoolgirl, full of fun, bubbling over with the joy of life, always the centre of attention. Somebody told me that you had not been well, something had happened! Some pain had proved too much, and your poor sensitive soul had taken refuge behind a closed, lonely door where nobody could reach you.

I longed to go and put my arms around you, and let you know that you are loved and cherished. Fear prevented me, however. Fear perhaps of rejection, but also I didn't want you to think that I was acting out of pity. So I asked the Lord to assure you somehow that no pain is too great for the power of His love to erase. I asked Him to make you conscious of the strength of His strong arm which is gently guiding you out into the light again.

JIM, WHO SUFFERED from depression over a number of years, used the above words from *Les Miserables* to explain the bleak misery of the awful suffering he went through during that period of his life. At first, he was ignoring the symptoms; the lack of concentration, confusion, gradual withdrawal from people, lack of interest, overeating, smoking too much, not returning phone calls, not opening letters, letting dirty laundry pile up; thoughts of suicide, fear of leaving the house, fear of staying in; taking to bed as an escape.

'I was caught up in thinking constantly, involuntarily, about hopelessness, fear and dread; this took all my waking hours. I wanted to get out of my head but couldn't.'

Those who suggested that he 'pull himself together' just didn't understand that he was unable to.

Eventually, Jim overcame his depression, with a great deal of help and a period in hospital. Today he counsels sufferers and assures them that there is life after depression. 'It may take time but the waiting is worth it; there is life on the other side.'

He also points to the loneliness of Jesus and His desperate cry of abandonment on the cross, which is still heard in the voices of all who suffer. But, remember, he says, that cry was heard. And all who have entered the pit and touched the wounds of Jesus have met and come to know more intimately Thomas Merton's 'Christ of the burnt men'.

LEAD KINDLY LIGHT

Lead, kindly light, amid the encircling gloom,
Lead Thou me on;
The night is dark, and I am far from home,
Lead Thou me on.
Keep Thou my feet: I do not ask to see
The distant scene; – one step enough for me.

I was not ever thus, nor prayed that Thou
Should lead me on;
I loved to choose and see my path; but now –
Lead Thou me on.
I loved the garish day; and, spite of fears,
Pride ruled my will; – remember not past years.

So long Thy power hath blest me, sure it still
Will lead me on –
O'er moor and fell, o'er crag and torrent, till
The night is gone –
And with the morn those angel-faces smile
Which I have loved long since, and lost awhile.

CARDINAL J. H. NEWMAN

♥

THE CHALLENGE OF LOVING

Smiles can be deceptive: charm a deceiver.
A face apparently sincere can tell a thousand lies.

Sincerity and truth are rare today
Yet, the search for truth is the deepest craving
Of the human heart.

Can we really trust; become vulnerable.
Will we be broken and bent like the reed –
Left to straighten ourselves out
But never quite straight again.

Frailly we flutter in the wind
And join in the game of deception.
Bent and broken.

Our smile must also become deceptive
To disguise the fact that we are weeping inside.

YOUTH

YOUTH ROLE MODEL

The lyrics of a song I heard recently on radio, went something like this: 'Bad wisdom – too much, too soon, and now I am paying the price with my body for bad wisdom!' The sad cry of today's young AIDS victims, drug and alcohol abusers, abortion and suicide victims. All paying, with their bodies and their lives, for the 'bad wisdom' with which they are being exploited by our world.

They need good 'models', people whom they can admire and relate to – who can present an alternative to them, guides who can lead them away from the quagmire of our shoddy secular society, into the realisation of the light and beauty of God's love.

Undoubtedly, one of the finest models for the youth of our age, is someone who lived in a world very similar to our own. Who, as a young man, was also caught up in the allure of pleasure and self-seeking, which was part and parcel of the erotic culture of the society in which he lived. His name is St Augustine of Hippo, one of the greatest saints of all time.

Augustine, who was born in the year 354 in North Africa, moved to Rome as a young man and became entangled, to an extent, in the allurements of that society. God's presence was denied and pushed aside, in that world of the then crumbling Roman Empire in which Augustine lived and taught. But Augustine waded through the sham and hypocrisy in search of the Truth, and after a long and very painful search, through many of the wrong areas, he ultimately found God. And this is the story that he has to tell to the youth of our age, who are experiencing a similar struggle themselves.

Because he was such a gifted and prolific writer and communicator – he wrote over 230 books, nearly 300 letters of his are preserved and about 400 sermons – the wisdoms and counsels of his 'towering intellect' speak to us across the centuries with the grace, warmth and clarity that captivated and spoke to the hearts of his listeners during his lifetime. He held people enthralled with his powerful personality and his gifted use of words and expressions. He could move his congregation both to laughter and tears with his warmth and wit. He didn't care how – and we are told that he often sacrificed grammar and eloquence – his purpose was to reach people and plant the Word of God in their hearts.

For, having found God, he was so overjoyed and appreciative, he just couldn't stop himself, it seems, from sharing Him with everybody else! Nobody is drawn to God by force, Augustine believed. God's love does not 'wax and wane' according to our performance. Conversion comes through a realisation of God's unconditional love for us – we are drawn to Him by attraction.

His own story, told with so much warmth, clarity and almost naive honesty, in his *Confessions* has inspired and helped many to go 'that extra mile' on their journey towards God. 'For a mere sentence the words of St Augustine struck me with a power which I had never felt from any words before ...' said the late Cardinal John Henry Newman, shortly before he entered the Catholic Church. 'The physical man is with us, stirring us with his energy, and singeing us with his flame', wrote Robert Speaight.

St Augustine's story is the story of a relentless search for happiness – a happiness which kept eluding him. A brilliant scholar, he became a university professor – a master of rhetoric. He was extremely popular with friends and colleagues alike. He loved the theatre and music and somewhat in the mode of the times, took a mistress, who bore him a son, whom he adored. But Augustine still had not found happiness. And so, like someone climbing a great mountain determined to reach the summit, he continued to search for that 'something better'.

He wrote that he was being carried along by a love of investigating the truth – 'I had delight in truth, even in little things'. When you sincerely search for the Truth you will always find Him!

Father, I am seeking, I am hesitant and uncertain,
But will you, O Lord, watch over each step of mine,

70

And guide me.

After his conversion, he turned around and related the whole experience in his *Confessions*.

This book has been called one of the greatest spiritual classics of all time. What Augustine manages to achieve reminds me a little of the Gospel story on the Road to Emmaus. In his *Confessions* he invites the reader to walk every step of the road with him. He doesn't rush ahead, he is the companion sharing all the deepest cries and fears of his 'restless' yearnings. So that at the moment of his famous conversion, one is actually part of his boundless joy – and the 'treasure' he finds becomes everyone's 'pearl beyond price'. Throughout the centuries many people said they had found a friend for life at the conclusion of the book!

Fr Gervase Corcoran, OSA, one of this country's foremost authorities on Augustine today, tells us, he believed that love was the most important thing in human life: 'Love beginning is perfection beginning, love growing is perfection growing, complete love is complete perfection'.

There was always a vague sadness about him, even in his youth, one of his greatest fears, for example, was the fear of losing friends. He wrote: 'When ever a man is without a friend not a single thing in the world appears friendly to him'.

Insensitivity was high on his list of moral defects: 'If apatheia (apathy) is the name of the state in which the mind cannot be touched by any emotion whatsoever, who would not judge this insensitivity to be the worst of all moral defects?'

Fundamentally an artist, Augustine was above all else 'A Man of the Heart', says Fr Corcoran. This is why the warmth of his oftimes 'bleeding and bruised' heart can reach us today across the centuries, because the language of the heart is not confined by the bonds of time. He is the perfect illustration of Vauvenargues' maxim that 'Great thoughts spring from the Heart!'

St Augustine, fired by a thirst for life which earthly existence could not satisfy, urges us on through this earthly struggle, never hoping for perfection, but through our 'fits and starts', our mistakes and imperfections, we may come to the realisation, as he did, that: 'You have made us for Yourself O Lord, and our hearts are restless until they rest in Thee'.

When my whole being is united with You,
Then I will feel no more sorrow or pain ...
You are the doctor, I am the patient
You are the giver of mercy, I am in great need of it.

St Augustine

YOUTH OUR MOST PRECIOUS COMMODITY

Our most precious and most important 'commodity' is our youth. Their future, their happiness, the type of world they inherit should be our prime concern and should come first in our list of priorities ahead of our commercial interests and our power struggles. They look to us for a sense of values, a sense of direction in a world which is largely exploiting them.

What they need most of all is love, encouragement, a sense of purpose in life – a challenge to bring out and put into practice their fundamental goodness. They need to be told that their value does not depend on how many points they get, or their popularity among their peers – that their value and their dignity comes from the fact that they are individually and uniquely loved by God.

What type of society are we helping to create for them? Is it a society based on Christian values, or are we accepting the standards being introduced through the medium of films, TV, videos, etc., which appeal to the lower side of human nature, and tear down rather than build up the fabric of society. By and large the media are promoting a pleasure seeking culture and the victims are largely our youth — the statistics of abortions, alcohol and drug abusers, AIDS victims tell the sad tale!

The media has enormous power to influence our world, with this power comes an awesome responsibility. There are, however, individuals working within the structure who are courageously and consistently seeking to improve and build up the fabric of society. One such person is film director David Puttnam, he believes the film industry has a responsibility to educate audiences to become better human beings. In his films, *The Killing Fields*, *The Mission* and *Chariots of Fire*, he sets out to do just that – he presents a character who is deeply committed to acting out a principle and feels accountable to act and change society for the better. The fact that he has received so many Oscar awards, for these films proves that there are many decent, like-minded people interested in making a case for a better society.

Each of us in our own way can do our bit to make this a better world for our young people to inherit. Our children are a special gift from God. He places His precious little ones in our care to be loved and nurtured. They are not our possessions, they belong to Him ultimately – we only get a loan of them for a little time.

This country is blessed with the largest number of young people in Europe at present – let us love and treasure them enough to fight for a better world for them.

Our happiness, my dears, is in the power One who can bring it about in a thousand unforeseen ways that mock our foresight.

OLIVER GOLDSMITH

FROM THE HEART ...

A worried mother whose son failed to gain enough points to enter third level education, was distraught: 'But what is he going to do,' she moaned, 'how will he ever get anywhere now!'

The points system piles a heavy burden on the shoulders of the young, putting them under dreadful pressure. If they don't get the number of points they need they can feel that they have failed to measure up to what is expected of them, or that they are not clever enough or capable of keeping up with their peers. Parents worry equally if their child doesn't succeed in the points 'rat race'. They worry about their prospects for the future when the doors of third-level institutions have been closed to them.

However, some of the greatest statesmen, writers, artists, entrepreneurs, composers, inventors, people in every walk of life, were not achievers at school.

The great American inventor, Thomas Edison, who was awarded the Nobel prize for physics, in 1915, only spent three months of his life at school. His teacher thought him stupid, so his mother took him away and taught him herself, encouraging his one predominant desire – which was to learn how everything 'worked'.

The Curé of Ars, patron saint of priests, had great difficulty learning Latin and almost failed to be accepted for ordination. The first pope was a humble fisherman and a large number of the saints were not scholars.

Education in the broadest sense, means the art of training the mind and character and also teaching the techniques that will enable pupils to earn their livelihood, make use of their own special talents, and be good and fruitful members of the community. This broad vision, whereby students need nurturing and encouragement to help them to grow into happy and caring human beings and to develop their own unique skills and gifts, is being stunted by the pressure on both pupils and teachers to produce ever higher exam grades.

In that lovely children's song 'There are so many colours in the rainbow', we are given a glimpse of the wonderfully creative mind of a little child struggling to reach beyond the confines of a system which curbs the beauty of his creative vision.

One of the happiest households I know, revolves around a little mentally impaired child. The love and affection which exudes from this child, not only towards family members, but towards the many visitors to that house, is a joy to behold.

Similarly, in the L'Arche communities, where a number of mentally impaired people live with others who do not suffer from what we term 'a mental handicap' – the atmosphere is charged with love and affection. And the helpers insist that they receive far more than they are capable of giving.

God has created each little child uniquely special and very precious to Him. We have to accept that He has a plan for each one, which is very often far removed from our world's narrow and stilted vision for them.

If a man does not keep pace with his companions,
Perhaps it is because he hears a different drummer.
Let him step to the music he hears,
However measured or far away.

THOREAU

LOVE ASKS NO RETURN

As the little swallow can be battered and damaged by a severe storm, so can a little child whose experience of life has been unstable and turbulent.

The teacher introduced me to little Sally – a lovely smiling happy little girl, who proudly performed the one-act play which she had been taught. When she had finished the other children clapped and applauded, and Sally returned to her seat pleased as punch.

She had been very disruptive in class at first, the teacher explained. 'She really did try my patience. But then I discovered that the poor little mite had spent most of her young life moving from one temporary foster home to another, and I recognised that what she was really craving was love and affirmation.

'But her behaviour, of course, was sending out all the wrong messages, and instead of receiving what she needed most of all, she was pushing people away through her conduct. Her classmates didn't want to play with her because she was overly boisterous with them, so she generally ended up on her own during break time – a lonely little figure sucking her thumb!'

The teacher decided that she would have to try to find some means through which she could encourage Sally and build her confidence. She wasn't achieving at all in any of the academic areas, so she would have to find something outside of the books for which she could justifiably receive praise and acclaim. Eventually she came up with an idea. Sally was a born actress with a lovely singing voice, so she encouraged her to take the lead in the Christmas play. That was the breakthrough! From that day on she gradually built up confidence in herself and got good grades in her class work. Slowly, but surely, she began to thrive, to get on well with her schoolmates and now, many months later, she was a totally different child – happy and contented.

Sally was lucky, she found someone who cared enough to love and encourage her and draw out her gifts and the best that was in her.

As she told her story, the teacher didn't realise the light of love which shone in her face for her little charge!

The Lord places someone in need of being 'put together again' in our path every day and tells us 'As often as you did it to one of these, the least of my brethren, you did it to me!'

FAITH

GOOD SHEPHERD NEVER DESERTS HIS FLOCK

'When deer have to cross a river, each one of them carries on its back the head of the one following, while it rests its head on the back of the one preceding. In this way, supporting and helping each other, they are able to cross safely wide rivers, until they reach the stability of land'. St Augustine uses this lovely example from the animal kingdom to illustrate the meaning of Christianity in practice. The Church is a body of people, committed to Christ and His ideal of love, travelling through this world towards our home in heaven.

On our journey we try to bring Jesus's love, compassion and kindness to those we meet on the way. We try to take on His values and attitudes. Like the deer, we lean and depend on Him to carry and support us through the crosses and trials of life and recognise His hand in the love and compassion we receive from others in our darkest moments.

He came to serve and His rule of love is service. To illustrate this He refers to Himself as the Good Shepherd who is constantly with his flock. He cares for them day and night, bandages the wounded, heals those who are sick, leaves the whole flock to go after the one who wandered off and brings him back again on His shoulders. This supreme hero will take on any enemy who dares to attack his sheep. He is prepared to give His very life for any one of them to prove how much He loves and cares for them. And this is exactly what He did!

This story is not a myth or a fable. It is the root and source of Christ's Church on earth. It is the reason why the Gospel message is called 'The Good News'. Because that is what it is. The knowledge of this message has the power to drive out all fear and anxiety and fill us with hope and confidence. We are very special, guarded like the apple of His eye, our names are written on the palms of His hand and the very hairs of our head are numbered. 'Do not be afraid little flock', Jesus counsels us, when the storms of this life are raging and threatening.

He is in the eye of the storm. He is in charge.

Because of what is happening in our society at present we have to go to the source of truth and love to find direction and guidance. The shock announcements which are appearing on a daily basis, of sin and corruption, are creating a great deal of fear and unease. People are scandalised, angry and sad. It appears that the very structures of our society are crumbling and that the institutions upon which we relied are no longer secure.

However, something good is emerging out of all the confusion and pain. New life is emerging.

Because the existence of God has been denied and pushed aside by some sectors of our society, a new need is emerging and that is the need for justice and truth. This search for truth is a very good thing, but what is not so good about the present relentless exposure of those found or assumed to be guilty, is that very little mercy is being shown. Truth and justice will always stand side-by-side with mercy. Because God is truth, mercy is His most outstanding quality. If we present sinners in an unmerciful way, as bait for the pack of wolves, we are denying the fact that we are all sinners. 'Let the one who is without sin cast the first stone'.

Any genuine search for truth must begin with ourselves, we must find it first in our own hearts. Otherwise if we only go outside in search of truth, we may be searching for a weapon that will humiliate and destroy. And those who pretend to use truth in this way are not being truthful people.

Christ entrusted His Church into the care of other shepherds and appointed them to lead and care for his flock. These were a band of ordinary men, one of whom even betrayed Him, but the others, with one exception, gave their lives for Him.

'Never judge the majority by the misbehaviour of a few', said Cardinal Basil Hume, praising priests for their heroic work in a world which too often shows no appreciation for their 'untold and unsung' dedication.

Christ was never slow to admonish and correct injustice, and it is false charity to remain silent in the face of blatant wrong, both for the sake of the offender and the victim. However, God commands us to love even our enemies, and to show compassion to the greatest sinner. We must respect the dignity of every human being. Everybody must be given the opportunity of repenting and reforming. Christ alone knows the heart. He alone understands the evil/or sickness that drives people to harm and damage others, or to become obsessed with power or greed.

It is said that we can only do good when we are loved. The greatest Christian charity is to love the unloved and unlovable. The sinner needs to meet Christ, as the Good Thief did. Christ asks us to become His healing face. St Theresa, the Little Flower, made it her vocation 'to be love'. The only distinguishable mark of a Christian is love.

Someone said, it is not enough to say we love God we must prove it. Faith is not faith at all until it is tested. We all share responsibility for the mending and cleansing needed to stop the rot in our society. The apathy, what we have failed to do in justice and love, has certainly contributed to the present problems. 'All it takes for evil to prosper is for good men to remain silent'. The evil of the world has always attacked the good and has always been present. It is constantly at play within each of us. But we are assured that the power of prayer combats all evil.

Oliver Goldsmith pointed out that our happiness is in 'the power of One who can bring it about in a thousand unforeseen ways that mock our foresight'.

Christ, the Good Shepherd, is guiding and leading His Church – the people of God – He always will! Pain and suffering always give way to new life. And He forbids us to worry.

'Courage, fear not ... I have overcome the world'.

He loves each one of us as if there were only one of us.

St Augustine

Be — Attitudes

Our attitudes, what we think, what we do and how we behave towards each other, is what we are. If we are loving, caring, kind and just, we will automatically bring these qualities to bear in our dealings with others and in each of our actions.

In His Sermon on the Mount, Jesus asks us to take on the attitude of kindness, gentleness, justice, forgiveness, mercy and compassion. He said 'I thirst' for my people if they thirst, if they are lonely, hungry, oppressed, so whatever you do for them you do for me!

Love

We are to love one another, as He loves us. The early Christians were distinguishable by the love they showed towards one another. 'See these Christians how they love one another'.

Love comes from God, He is the author, the source of love. The only way we can love with His love is to stay very close to Him, like a tap which serves no useful purpose until it is turned on, but then becomes the means through which water can flow. So must we 'cleave' to Christ, as close as the vine is to the branches, if we are to become the channels through which His love flows out to touch the lives of others. Left to our own human condition, our love will always be conditional and somewhat lacking.

The first of the Beatitudes puts it all in perspective, which is that we should know our need of God.

Love is patient and kind; it is not jealous or conceited or proud; love is not ill-mannered or selfish or irritable; love does not keep a record of wrongs; love is not happy with evil, but is happy with

the truth. Love never gives up; and its faith, hope and patience
will never fail. (I Cor. 13:4–8).

GENEROSITY/KINDNESS

In the Old Testament God points out that He does not want
'empty sacrifices' whilst the poor and oppressed, the widows
and orphans go uncared for.

At the end of Mass we are asked to go out and put into
practice what we have just professed.

Have you met God's love today, I asked a little child?
Have you met His love I enquired of the lonely old man?
I asked the poor bedraggled old woman pushing her trolley
    around the streets.
I asked the boy with AIDS.
The young mother with cancer.
The unemployed, disillusioned girl.
The bereaved widow.
The one suffering from drug addiction.
Yes, they told me, they had encountered His love.
Somebody had been kind, somebody had been generous and
    caring, somebody had given them their time!

Little children, let us not love with the word, neither with the
tongue, but in deed and in truth.

(Jn 1:3)

In the evening of our lives we will be judged on how we have loved.
St John of the Cross

GENTLENESS/MEEKNESS

Christ said: ' ... learn from me for I am gentle and humble in spirit' (Mt. 11.29).

It was a wet, cold, gloomy morning and my mood matched that of the weather. I was feeling frankly downcast when I met Nancy. She has the beautiful gift of being able to uplift people – with her cheerful smile and kindly manner, she lifts the heart of everybody with whom she comes into contact.

One of the greatest acts of love is encouragement. Our smile or word of encouragement can lift the burden of another and help remove the greyness and let the sunshine back into someone's life once again.

Christ asks us to be His smile and His kind word for everyone.

There is nothing as strong as gentleness and nothing as gentle as real strength.

St Francis de Sales

There will ever be a number of persons
too young to be wise
too generous to be cautious,
too warm to be sober,
or too intellectual to be humble.

Cardinal J. H. Newman

JUSTICE/TRUTH

In the clearing out of the money changers from the Temple, Christ gave us a very clear picture of His attitude towards those who would 'defile His Father's house'. Similarly, in His dealings with the scribes and pharisees He would seem to be very harsh with His comments, such as 'you hypocrites' and 'brood of vipers', etc., when He came up against hypocrisy or injustice. This was 'the gentle Jesus' who was strong enough and courageous enough to seek justice for all.

Most of us like to avoid conflict. One of the reasons is we like others to think well of us, or perhaps we don't want to incur someone's wrath, so we often stay silent. Many injustices in our society go unchecked because we do not have the courage to speak out against them.

Christ was not caught up in preserving a popular image. Truth and justice were His concerns and He was prepared to suffer the consequences of standing up to be counted in defence of both.

The Cure of Ars wrote: 'There is such a thing as a holy anger, which comes from our zeal in upholding the interests of God.' He also said 'The sun never hides its light for fear of inconveniencing the owls.'

Christ died for the truth, anyone who doesn't have the courage to stand up and be counted in defence of the truth cannot say they follow the One who was 'The Way, the Truth and the Life'.

This above all, to thine own self be true, and it must follow, as the night the day, thou can'st not then be false to any man.

SHAKESPEARE

FORGIVENESS/MERCY

Christians are followers of the One who begged for mercy for the people who were nailing Him to the Cross!

One of the greatest stumbling blocks and most difficult challenges of all, is that we forgive from our hearts those who have hurt and injured us; Those who have no love only contempt and hatred for us, even those who would destroy us.

Jesus tells us we must forgive not only seven times, but seventy times seven. 'Be good to those who hate you, bless those who curse you and pray for those who persecute you.'

At first this may even seem an unjust request, surely, we might argue, people who deliberately set out to harm others shouldn't be allowed to get away with it? But as each of Christ's counsels stem from His love and wisdom – nothing is more important to the health of both our souls and bodies than our need to forgive and be forgiven.

In Charles Dickens *Great Expectations*, we see the lonely, sad figure of Miss Havisham, the lady who, because of the deep hurt she experienced when her bridegroom rejected her on her wedding day, spent the remainder of her life encased in this hurt. In a word, it destroyed her. Had she found it in her heart to forgive, how different her story might have been!

When we either refuse to forgive, or feel unable to do so, it's we ourselves who suffer most, usually becoming hardhearted and bitter.

But our forgiveness is also essential for the one who has injured us. It is said that one can only do good when one is loved. When we react with love instead of 'an eye for an eye and a tooth for a tooth', we enable the wrongdoer to change and become better. Just as forgiveness frees us from a deep pit of our own hurt so does it free the one who has scarred us. Because when someone is caught up in causing harm and suffering to others, it is they themselves who are hurting inside.

But, as Oliver Goldsmith says, it takes more than human benevolence to do this. It takes a kind of superhuman effort and as we are incapable of accomplishing it on our own, we need Christ's help to do so. With this command, He provides us with the means!

♥

The quality of mercy is not strain'd;
It droppeth, as the gentle rain from heaven,
Upon the place beneath; it is twice bless'd –
It blesseth him that gives, and him that takes;
'Tis mightiest in the mightiest; it becomes
The throned monarch better than his crown;
His sceptre shews the force of temporal power,
The attribute to awe and majesty,
Wherein doth sit the dread and fear of kings;
But mercy is above this sceptr'd sway,
It is an attribute to God Himself;
And earthly power doth then shew likest God's,
When mercy seasons justice. Therefore, Jew,
Though justice be thy plea, consider this –
That in the course of justice, none of us
Should see salvation. We do pray for mercy;
And that same prayer doth teach us all to render
The deeds of mercy. I have spoke thus much
To mitigate the justice of the plea;
Which if thou follow, this strict court of Venice
Must needs give sentence 'gainst the merchant there.

THE MERCHANT OF VENICE, SHAKESPEARE

LETTING GO

Recently I decided to redecorate a room. Before I could get around to the business of painting and cleaning, however, I had to sift through all the paraphernalia of books, papers, letters, photographs and all sorts of odds and ends, which I had accumulated over a period of time. The most difficult part was trying to decide what to keep and what to get rid of. We become attached to things for sentimental reasons, or we may want to hold on to them feeling that they may be useful some day. On this occasion, however, I decided that if I was to achieve what I set out to do, which was to have a nice clean, orderly room once again, then I would just have to let go of most of what I had hoarded.

Isn't this what happens in our lives? On a day to day basis, we can adopt bad habits and wrong attitudes, without being fully conscious of what we are doing. We can get caught up in a power or an ego trip; in undermining or 'walking over' others in order to achieve our own interests; or just become so engrossed with our own needs that we fail to offer a helping hand to those whose burdens are heavier than our own.

We need to stop every now and then and take stock, to ask ourselves the all important question – 'where are we going?' If we believe in God and in the hereafter, how are we preparing for it? When we come to meet God at the end of our life here on earth, will it be with a sense of remorse and regret that we didn't try to build up a friendship with Him when we had the opportunity, or because we didn't try to do His will while on earth?

In St Teresa of Avila's *Interior Castle,* she likens the soul to a castle in which there are many rooms. In describing the journey inwards towards the centre, where God is, she shows how we have to do a stock-take in each of the rooms, which means letting go of more and more, before we can move to a deeper level, closer to God.

As St John of the Cross says all we will have at the end of our lives is what we have given away!

A MEDITATION

CARDINAL NEWMAN

God has created me to do Him some definite service. He has committed some work to me which He has not committed to another. I have my mission. I may never know it in this world. But I shall be told it in the next.

I am a link in the chain. A bond of connection between persons. He has not created me for naught. I shall do good. I shall do His work. I shall be an angel of peace. A preacher of truth in my own place, while not intending it. If I do but keep His commandments.

Therefore I will trust Him. Wherever, whatever I am, I can never be thrown away. If I am in sickness, my sickness may serve Him; in perplexity, my perplexity may serve Him; if I am in sorrow, my sorrow may serve Him.

He does nothing in vain. He knows what He is about. He may take away my friends, He may throw me among strangers. He may make me feel desolate, make my spirits sink, hide my future from me ... still ... He knows what He is about.

PRAYER IS SIMPLY LOVING GOD

Her life revolves around a large number of people world-wide. Every day she sets about helping those who are in trouble. Those most in need are the focus of her special attention.

She forms a list in her mind: the prisoner bound for execution, the person closest to despair, the one undergoing torture, the abandoned child , the suicidal. She enters the lives of people in every corner of the globe.

Hers is an amazingly challenging life. Never a dull

moment she confesses, because there are so many people in need at any given moment.

Prayer is 'the tool' through which she enters the lives of those she serves in love. You see, she lives in a hospital ward, on the flat of her back. She will never meet those 'friends' she helps with so much love!

BETTY, WHO LIVES in the same hospital, is upset and agitated because due to her illness, she is unable to pray she says. 'I just can't pray, I try and try but I can't concentrate – I can't even say the Rosary.

Betty suffers a great deal of pain, but never utters a word of complaint 'Oh, I offer it up – I look at the crucifix and feel that I have nothing to complain about compared to what Jesus had to suffer.'

Prayer, we are assured, is simply loving God. We could be babbling off prayers like a gymnast, but if we don't put love into them we might as well be doing gymnastics!

That is why Christ asked us to pray from the heart – we unite our hearts to the Sacred Heart of Jesus, and He sees all that is in them. That is all.

Prayer is someone, not something.

Prayer is about approaching a loving father with the guileless trust and confidence of a child

Little Brian couldn't get his father's attention. He pulled at his trouser leg, his father absently responded but did not take his eyes off his paper. Johnny tried again this time stamping his feet and screaming – no response! Refusing to give up, he climbed up on to his father's lap, and caught his face between his two chubby little hands. He then turned his father's face towards him and held it there, thereby receiving his father's full attention.

This is what happens when we pray. This is how Our Father wants us to approach Him, with the trust and confidence of a small child approaching a loving father.

Prayer is about friendship

'Look,' said little Johnny's mother, pointing to the picture of the Sacred Heart, 'look at the light shining on His poor sore hands!' Little Johnny understood, and I felt sure that he would remember this lesson on prayer because it was spoken from the heart, and children live in the heart.

All prayer starts from a desire to pray, it is an attitude of the heart, a bridge which links us with God. Nothing could be simpler, as Christ pointed out to His disciples when they asked Him to teach them to pray. He began by telling them what not to do. They did not need to use lots of words, and they were not to follow the example of the hypocrites who loved to pray in public.

Christ Himself is the internal teacher of prayer, so we do not have to worry, if we just have the desire to cross that bridge, if we are prepared to let go and just put one step forward He will lead us across.

Prayer links us to God in friendship, it is a reaching out on our part to grasp the strong warm hand which He holds out to us. The quality of our prayer will depend on the trust and hope which we place in Him.

Prayer is a coping mechanism

Lord Tennyson, the poet, pointed out that 'more things are wrought by prayer than this world dreams of' and many people are discovering that it is 'the most powerful force on earth'.

One young man discovered the power of prayer in his life at a time when he was very depressed and was actually contemplating suicide.

'I now carry this safety valve about with me,' Seán said, 'like a cordless phone – it's my direct line to God! I check in first thing in the morning, just to remind Him that I am on the line,' he smiles. 'When you have stood on the brink of suicide, you are aware of your own weakness, so I ask Him to stay with me throughout the day and throughout the night – I know that He does, and I am not afraid anymore – prayer is my coping mechanism.'

THERE ARE SOME PEOPLE who will say that they have tried prayer but that God didn't answer them, and so they become angry with Him and turn away. When we really come to the realisation of the largeness of God, of the boundless depth of His love and compassion we will surely come to realise that He always gives us what we really need.

Prayer nearly always starts from pain and suffering. It is not surprising that the cross is the mark of Christianity, because it is only by keeping our eyes fixed on Christ on the cross that we begin to cope with the mystery of suffering. Christ on His cross should be our model whatever we may have to endure.

A friend of mine loves to point out that 'God is a gentleman, he never goes where he isn't invited'. In Holman Hunt's picture *Light of the World*, we see Jesus with a lantern in His hand knocking at a door which has no handle on the outside. The door to the room where Christ dwells within us can only be opened by ourselves.

If we decide to open this door we will discover love Himself. Through meditating on Christ's life we will begin to change and take on His attitudes. We will begin to move from selfishness to selflessness. He will teach us how to give until it hurts, how to love the people who make life difficult for us and give us strength to cope, no matter how difficult we may be finding life.

THE TOUCH OF HIS HAND

Did you sleep well last night, or did you spend the night tossing and turning, unable to catch those much needed 40 winks.

Sheila, who has a lot of problems, more than seems fair for any one person to have to carry, told me how she devised a means of coping with sleeplessness. As she lay awake for the third successive night, she decided that she would have to learn some method of coping with the problem – 'otherwise I knew that I was going to become addicted to the sleeping pills, the bottle or whatever.'

Sheila's decision was to concentrate on all the good and uplifting things that had happened during the day: each little kindness, the sound of a little bird singing outside her window, a telephone call from a friend, a smile from someone on the street. 'Since God is in all the good things, I decided to concentrate on each and every good thing that had permeated my day and I was amazed to find all the "little miracles" which I realised were God's comforting and consoling love. These were His way of letting me know that He was caring for me. I felt the touch of His hand, and saw that He was right there with me all the time!

We cannot help feeling low and depressed at times. We cannot help it when life's problems weigh heavily on our shoulders, but we can take a decision to do something about it.

Christ wants us to be happy, and over and over again, He asks us not to allow ourselves to become bogged down with anxiety and worry: 'Do not be afraid, little flock ... Every hair of your head is numbered ... I have written your name on the palms of my hands ... You are worth more than many sparrows ... Fear not, I have overcome the world ... Cast all your cares on Me.' We must, as Sheila has done, recognise the touch of His hand in all the goodness and beauty which enters our lives every day.

Let nothing disturb you
Nothing frighten you
All things are passing
God never changes.

Patience achieves all things
He who has God finds he lacks nothing,
God alone suffices.

ST TERESA OF AVILA

MORE INTERESTING BOOKS

SOMETHING UNDERSTOOD

A SPIRITUAL ANTHOLOGY

EDITED BY SEÁN DUNNE

This anthology contains a rich selection of writing on many aspects of spirituality. They include God, pain, prayer, love, loss, joy and silence. Drawing on the great tradition of Christian Spirituality, Seán Dunne has assembled pieces by dozens of writers, among them Thomas Merton, Simone Weil, Teresa of Avila, John Henry Newman and Dietrich Bonhoeffer. He has also chosen from the work of creative writers such as Patrick Kavanagh, John McGahern, Kate O'Brien and George Herbert. With a wide selection of material that ranges from just a few lines to many pages, *Something Understood* is a perfect source for reflection on aspects of spirituality that have been the concern of men and women through the centuries.

THE SPIRIT OF
TONY DE MELLO

A HANDBOOK OF MEDIATION EXERCISES

JOHN CALLANAN, SJ

This book captures the essence and spirit of Tony de Mello. He was a great teacher. Some said he was a dangerous one. He constantly challenged himself, the world within which he lived and those he came into contact with. For some this element of challenge was both unsettling and confusing. Tony said that our security does not lie in thoughts or ideas no matter how profound. Neither does it lie in traditions – no mattered how hallowed. Security can only reside in an attitude of mind and a readiness to reflect deeply, thus subjecting any and every belief to rigorous questioning.

So Tony urged people to question, question question. Questions often make us uncomfortable. They do, however, force us to reflect and thus ensure our growth.

John Callanan has started the book with an opening chapter on the basics of prayer. Then he moves on to try and give a flavour of the ideas and themes which gave so much zest and life to Tony de Mello's presentations. The exercises in this book are based on the prayer-style which Tony himself developed during his retreats.